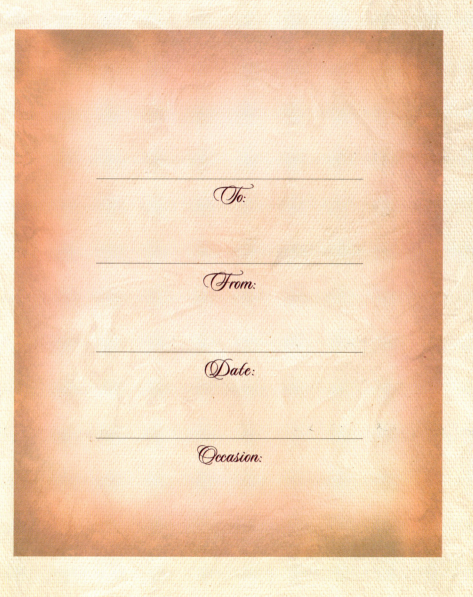

To:

From:

Date:

Occasion:

YOUR GIFT OF

Love

by

Gary Chapman, Ph.D.

YOUR GIFT OF

Love

Selections From The Five Love Languages

by

Gary Chapman, Ph.D.

C O N T

E N T S

A Note from Gary

Love is the most important word in the English language, and the most confusing. Marital intimacy is the by-product of meeting each other's emotional need for love. Obviously thousands of couples have failed at this endeavor. In order to be a successful lover, one must first learn the fundamentals. After twenty-five years as a marriage counselor, I think I have learned the essential insights in giving and receiving marital love. *Your Gift of Love* is my effort to share these insights in a concise, but hopefully compelling manner. Let's start at the beginning.

Love is always a gift. A gift implies grace, unmerited favor. If I offer love because someone has been kind to me, it ceases to be a gift and becomes payment for services rendered, and thus no longer love. True giving is found in loving people more than they deserve. Man's deepest longing is to feel truly loved. The most profound words ever written about God are the simple words, "God is love." Man is most god-like when he is loving.

In marriage, the person we would most like to love us is our spouse. In fact, if we feel loved, the whole world looks bright, but if not, our world becomes bleak. Meeting each other's emotional need for love is the key to a successful marriage. Keep love alive and the marriage will flourish. Remove love, and marriage wilts like a flower without water.

Meeting your spouse's need for love requires constant watering. The "in love" experience is temporary, designed simply to get us started. True love is intentional and often costly. First, it requires learning your spouse's "love language" — what makes him/her feel loved. Second, we must learn to speak that language, and third, we must speak their "love language" often.

My experience in marriage counseling has convinced me that there are only five basic love languages. Out of these five, each of us has a "primary" love language. My primary language is what really makes me feel loved. When my spouse speaks this language, my "love tank" fills rapidly. However, when my spouse fails to speak my love language, I will feel unloved, even though he/she may be trying to give me love in other languages.

Once my spouse is speaking my primary love language regularly, then the other four languages can be "icing on the cake," but without my primary language, there will be no cake. Many couple are sincere. They are expressing love to each other, but they are failing to connect emotionally, because they are not speaking each others "primary love language." Their marriage is filled with "icing," but the cake is missing.

In these marriages the following thoughts roll around in her mind: "If he loved me he would . . . . How could he be so uncaring? I thought he loved me, but I certainly don't feel loved." While he is asking himself: "Why doesn't she feel loved? Look what I did! Most women would be glad to have a husband like me. I don't understand her." Therein lies the problem: We don't understand each other.

This book will introduce you to the five basic love languages and help you discover the primary love language of your spouse. You will be able to meet your spouse's emotional need for love more effectively. You will learn how to invest your gift of love in a love language that will speak most deeply to your spouse. Hundreds of thousands of couples who have applied the principles of this book have reported: "The five love languages radically enhanced the emotional climate in our marriage." It is my sincere desire that you will find similar results in your marriage, and that you will share the message of *Your Gift of Love* with your friends. Love is life's most powerful gift.

INTRODUCTION

With all the books, magazines, and practical help available, why is it that so few couples seem to have found the secret to keeping love alive after the wedding? Why is it that a couple can attend a communication workshop, hear wonderful ideas on how to enhance communication, return home, and find themselves totally unable to implement the communication patterns demonstrated? How is it that we read a magazine article on "101 Ways to Express Love to Your Spouse," select two or three ways that seem especially good to us, try them, and our spouse doesn't even acknowledge our effort? We give up on the other 98 ways and go back to life as usual.

The answer to those questions is the purpose of this book. It is not that the books and articles already published are not helpful. The problem is that we have overlooked one fundamental truth: People speak different love languages.

WE MUST BE

WILLING TO LEARN

OUR SPOUSE'S

PRIMARY LOVE

LANGUAGE IF WE

ARE TO BE

EFFECTIVE

COMMUNICATORS

OF LOVE.

Most of us grow up learning the language of our parents and siblings, which becomes our primary or native tongue. Later, we may learn additional languages but usually with much more effort. These become our secondary languages. We speak and understand best our native language. We feel most comfortable speaking that language. The more we use a secondary language, the more comfortable we become conversing in it. If we speak only our primary language and encounter someone else who speaks only his or her primary language, which is different from ours, our communication will be limited. We must rely on pointing, grunting, drawing pictures, or acting out our ideas. We can communicate, but it is

Language of Love

awkward. Language differences are part and parcel of human culture. If we are to communicate effectively across cultural lines, we must learn the language of those with whom we wish to communicate.

Love need not evaporate, but in order to keep it alive most of us will have to put forth the effort to learn a secondary love language.

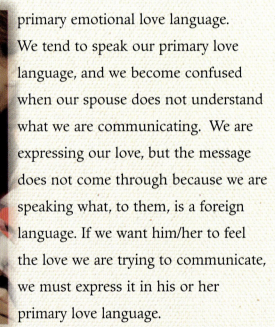

*P*oor parental programming does not mean that two people cannot communicate. But it does mean they will have to work at it more diligently than those who had a more positive model. Seldom do a husband and wife have the same primary emotional love language. We tend to speak our primary love language, and we become confused when our spouse does not understand what we are communicating. We are expressing our love, but the message does not come through because we are speaking what, to them, is a foreign language. If we want him/her to feel the love we are trying to communicate, we must express it in his or her primary love language.

AT THE HEART OF

MANKIND'S EXISTENCE

IS THE DESIRE TO

BE INTIMATE AND TO BE

LOVED BY ANOTHER.

intimacy

The need to feel loved by one's spouse is at the heart of marital desires. A man said, "What good is the house, the cars, the place at the beach, or any of the rest of it if your wife doesn't love you?" Do you understand what he was really saying? "More than anything, I want to be loved by my wife." Material things are no replacement for human, emotional love. A wife says, "He ignores me all day long and then wants to jump in bed with me. I hate it." She is not a wife who hates sex; she is a wife desperately pleading for emotional love. Something in our nature cries out to be loved by another. Marriage is designed to meet that need for intimacy and love.

2 Genuine Love

Welcome to the real world of marriage, where hairs are always on the sink and little white spots cover the mirror, where arguments center on which way the tissue paper comes off and whether the lid should be up or down. It is a world where shoes do not walk to the closet and drawers do not close themselves, where coats do not like hangers and socks go AWOL during laundry. In this world, a look can hurt and a word can crush. Intimate lovers can become enemies and marriage a battlefield.

Our most basic emotional need is not to fall in love but to be genuinely loved by another, to know a love that grows out of reason and choice, not instinct. I need to be loved by someone who chooses to love me, who

sees in me something worth loving. That kind of love requires effort and discipline—the choice to expend energy in an effort to benefit the other person, knowing that if his or her life is enriched by your effort, you too will find a sense of satisfaction—the satisfaction of having genuinely loved another.

Rational, volitional love . . . is the kind of love to which the sages have always called us.

The one who chooses to love will find appropriate ways to express that decision. "But it seems so sterile," some may contend. "Where are the shooting stars, the balloons, the deep emotions? What about the spirit of anticipation, the twinkle of the eye, the electricity of a kiss, the intimacy of sex? What about the emotional security of knowing that I am number one in his/her mind?"

How do we meet each other's deep, emotional need to feel loved? If we can learn that and choose to do it, then the love we share will be exciting beyond anything we ever felt when we were infatuated.

3 *Words of*

The object of love is not getting something you want but doing something for the well-being of the one you love. It is a fact, however, that when we receive affirming words we are far more likely to be motivated to reciprocate and do something our spouse desires.

Giving verbal compliments is only one way to express words of affirmation to your spouse. Another

dialect is encouraging words. The word encourage means "to inspire courage." All of us have areas in which we feel insecure. We lack

Your Gift of Love

Affirmation

courage, and that lack of courage often hinders us from accomplishing the positive things that we would like to do. The latent gifts, talents, and abilities within your spouse in his or her areas of insecurity may await your encouraging words.

MARK TWAIN ONCE SAID, "I CAN LIVE FOR TWO MONTHS ON A GOOD COMPLIMENT." IF WE TAKE TWAIN LITERALLY, SIX COMPLIMENTS A YEAR WOULD HAVE KEPT HIS EMOTIONAL LOVE TANK AT THE OPERATIONAL LEVEL. YOUR SPOUSE WILL PROBABLY NEED MORE.

*P*erhaps your spouse has untapped potential in one or more areas of life. That potential may be awaiting your encouraging words.

I am not talking about pressuring your spouse to do something that you want. I am talking about encouraging him to develop an interest that he already has. For example, some husbands pressure their wives to lose weight. The husband says, "I am encouraging her," but to the wife it sounds like condemnation. Only when a person wants to lose weight can you give her encouragement. Until she has the desire, your words will almost always be heard as words of judgment, designed to stimulate guilt. They express not love but rejection.

If, however, your spouse says, "I think I would like to enroll in a weight loss program this fall," then you have opportunity to give words of encouragement. Encouraging words would sound like this. "If you decide to do that, I can tell you one thing. You will be a success. That's one of the things I like about you. When you set your mind to something, you do it. If that's what you want to do, I will certainly do everything I can to help you. And don't worry about the cost of the program; we'll find the money." Such words may give your spouse the courage to phone the weight loss center.

ENCOURAGEMENT requires empathy and seeing the world from your spouse's perspective. We must first learn what is important to our spouse. Only then can we give encouragement. With verbal encouragement, we are trying to communicate, "I know. I care. I am with you. How can I help?" We are trying to show that we believe in him and in his abilities. We are giving credit and praise.

Most of us have more potential than we will ever develop. What holds us back is often courage. A loving spouse can supply that all-important catalyst. Of course, encouraging words may be difficult for you to speak. It may not be your primary love language. It may take great effort for you to learn this second language. That will be especially true if you have a pattern of critical and condemning words, but I can assure you that it will be worth the effort.

Love doesn't keep a score of wrongs. Love doesn't bring up past failures. None of us is perfect. In marriage we do not always do the best or right thing. We have sometimes done and said hurtful things to our spouses. We cannot erase the past. We can only confess it and agree that it was wrong. We can ask for forgiveness and try to act differently in the future. Having confessed my failure and asked forgiveness, I can do nothing more to mitigate the hurt it may have caused my spouse. When I have been wronged by my spouse and she has painfully confessed it and requested forgiveness, I have the option of justice or forgiveness. If I choose justice and seek to pay her back or make her pay for her wrongdoing, I am making myself the judge and her the felon. Intimacy becomes impossible. If, however, I choose to forgive, intimacy can be restored. Forgiveness is the way of love.

The object of love is not getting something you want but doing something for the wellbeing of the one you love. It is a fact, however, that when we receive affirming words we are far more likely to be motivated to reciprocate.

We cannot erase the past, but we can accept it as history. We can choose to live today free from the failures of yesterday. Forgiveness is not a feeling; it is a commitment. It is a choice to show mercy, not to hold the offense up against the offender. Forgiveness is an expression of love. "I love you. I care about you, and I choose to forgive you. Even though my feelings of hurt may linger, I will not allow what has happened to come between us. I hope that we can learn from this experience. You are not a failure because you have failed. You are my spouse, and together we will go on from here."

INTIMATE RELATIONSHIP, WE NEED TO

WISH TO LOVE EACH OTHER, WE NEED

PERSON WANTS.

Love makes requests, not demands. In marriage, we are equal, adult partners. If we are to develop an intimate relationship, we need to know each other's desires. If we wish to love each other, we need to know what the other person wants.

The way we express those desires, however, is all-important. If they come across as demands, we have erased the possibility of intimacy and will drive our spouse away. If, however, we make known our needs and desires as requests, we are giving guidance, not ultimatums.

When you make a request of your spouse, you are

affirming his or her worth and abilities. You are in

essence indicating that she has something or can do

something that is meaningful and worthwhile to you.

Love is always a choice. That's what makes it meaningful.

To know that my spouse loves me enough to respond to

one of my requests communicates emotionally that she

cares about me, respects me, admires me, and wants to

do something to please me.

4 Quality Time

Have you ever noticed that in a restaurant, you can almost always tell the difference between a dating couple and a married couple? Dating couples look at each other and talk. Married couples sit there and gaze around the restaurant. You'd think they went there to eat!

When I sit on the couch with my wife and give her twenty minutes of my undivided attention and she does the same for me, we are giving each other twenty minutes of life. We will never have those twenty minutes again; we are giving our lives to each other. It is a powerful emotional communicator of love.

A central aspect of quality time is togetherness, not just proximity. Togetherness has to do with focused attention.

Your Gift of Love

SOME HUSBANDS AND WIVES think they are spending time together when, in reality, they are only living in close proximity. They are in the same house at the same time, but they are not together. A husband who is watching sports on television while he talks to his wife is not giving her quality time, because she does not have his full attention.

Quality time does not mean that we have to spend our together moments gazing into each other's eyes. It means that we are doing something together and that we are giving our full attention to the other person. The activity in which we are both engaged is incidental. The important thing emotionally is that we are spending focused time with each other. The activity is a vehicle that creates the sense of togetherness. Our spending time together in a common pursuit communicates that we care about each other, that we enjoy being with each other, that we like to do things together.

relationship calls for sympathetic listening with a view to under- standing the other person's thoughts, feelings, and desires. Most of us have little training in listening. We are far more efficient in thinking and speaking. Learning to listen may be as difficult as learning a foreign language, but learn we must, if we want to communicate love.

Quality conversation requires not only sympathetic listening but also self-revelation. When a wife says, "I wish my husband would talk. I never know what he's thinking or feeling," she is pleading for intimacy. She wants to feel close to her husband, but how can she feel close to someone whom she doesn't know? In order for her to feel loved, he must learn to reveal himself. If her primary love language is quality time and her dialect is quality conversation, her emotional love tank will never be filled until he tells her his thoughts and feelings.

Many of us are trained
to analyze problems
and create solutions.
We forget that marriage
is a relationship, not a
project to be
completed
or a problem
to solve.

*S*elf-revelation does not come easy for some of us. Many adults grew up in homes where the expression of thoughts and feelings was not encouraged but condemned. By the time we reach adulthood, many of us have learned to deny our feelings. We are no longer in touch with our emotional selves.

A wife says to her husband, "How did you feel about what Don did?" And the husband responds, "I think he was wrong. He should have—" But he is not telling her his feelings. He is voicing his thoughts. Perhaps he has reason to feel angry, hurt, or disappointed, but he has lived so long in the world of thought that he does not acknowledge his feelings. When he

decides to learn the language of quality conversation, it will be like learning a foreign language. The place to begin is by getting in touch with his feelings, becoming aware that he is an emotional creature in spite of the fact that he has denied that part of his life.

When it comes to talking, I have observed two basic personality types. The first I call the "Dead Sea." This personality type receives many experiences, emotions, and thoughts throughout the day. They have a reservoir where they store information, and they are happy not to talk. If you say to a Dead Sea personality, "What's wrong? Why aren't you talking tonight?" he will probably answer, "Nothing's wrong. What makes you think something's wrong?" And that response is honest. He is content not to talk. He could drive from Chicago to Detroit and never say a word and be perfectly happy. On the other extreme is the "Babbling Brook." For this per-

ONE WAY TO LEARN NEW PATTERNS IS TO ESTABLISH A DAILY SHARING TIME IN WHICH EACH OF YOU WILL TALK ABOUT THREE THINGS THAT HAPPENED TO YOU THAT DAY AND HOW YOU FEEL ABOUT THEM.

sonality, whatever enters into the eye gate or the ear gate comes out the mouth gate. In fact if no one is at home to talk to, they will call someone else on the telephone.

If you are a Dead Sea and you date or marry a Babbling Brook, you don't have to think, "How will I get the conversation started tonight and keep it flowing?" In fact, you don't have to think at all. All you have to do is nod your head and say, "Uh huh," and she will fill up the whole evening. On the other hand, if you are a Babbling Brook and you date or marry a Dead Sea, you will have a wonderful time because Dead Seas are great listeners. You will babble; he will listen. You attract each other. But five years after marriage, the Babbling Brook wakes up one morning and says, "We've been married five years, and I don't know him." The Dead Sea is saying, "I know her too well. I wish she would stop the flow and give me a break." The good news is that Dead Seas can learn to talk and Babbling Brooks can learn to listen.

Your Gift of Love

$\mathcal{I}$n addition to the basic love language of quality time, or giving your spouse your undivided attention, is another dialect called quality activities. The emphasis is on being together, doing things together, and giving each other undivided attention.

Quality activities may include anything in which one or both of you has an interest. The emphasis is not on what you are doing but on why you are doing it. The purpose is to experience something together, to walk away from it feeling "He cares about me. He was willing to do something with me that I enjoy, and he did it with a positive attitude." That is love, and for some people it is love's loudest voice.

*Q*uality activities are limited only by your interest and willingness to try new experiences. The essential ingredients in a quality activity are:

(1) AT LEAST ONE OF YOU

WANTS TO DO IT,

(2) THE OTHER IS WILLING TO DO IT,

(3) BOTH OF YOU KNOW WHY YOU

ARE DOING IT—TO EXPRESS LOVE

BY BEING TOGETHER.

One of the by-products of quality activities is that they provide a memory bank from which to draw in the years ahead. Fortunate is the couple who remembers an early morning stroll along the coast, the time they got poison ivy chasing the rabbit through the woods, the night they attended their first major league baseball game together, the one and only time they went skiing together and he broke his leg, the amusement parks, the concerts, and oh, yes, the awe of standing beneath the waterfall after the two-mile hike. They can almost feel the mist as they remember. Those are memories of love, especially for the person whose primary love language is quality time.

5 Receiving Gifts

A gift is something you can hold in your hand and say, "Look, he was thinking of me," or, "She remembered me." You must be thinking of someone to give him a gift. The gift itself is a symbol of that thought. It doesn't matter whether it costs money. What is important is that you thought of him.

Mothers remember the days their children bring a flower from the yard as a gift. They feel loved, even if it was a flower they didn't want picked. From early years, children are inclined to give gifts to their parents, which may be another indication that gift giving is fundamental to love.

Gifts are visual symbols of love. Most wedding ceremonies include the giving and receiving of rings. The person performing the ceremony says, "These rings are outward and visible signs of an inward and spiritual bond that unites your two hearts in love that has no end." That is not meaningless rhetoric. It is verbalizing a significant truth—symbols have emotional value.

visual symbols of love

ifts may be purchased, found, or made. The husband who stops along the roadside and picks his wife a wildflower has found himself an expression of love, unless, of course, his wife is allergic to wildflowers. For the man who can afford it, you can purchase a beautiful card for less than five dollars. For the man who cannot, you can make one for free. Gifts need not be expensive.

But what of the person who says, "I'm not a gift giver. I didn't receive many gifts growing up. I never learned how to select gifts. It doesn't come naturally for me." Congratulations, you have just made the first discovery in becoming a great lover. You and your spouse speak different love languages. Now that you have made that discovery, get on with the business of learning your second language. If your spouse's primary love language is receiving gifts, you can become a proficient gift giver. In fact, it is one of the easiest love languages to learn.

If your spouse's primary love language is receiving gifts, you can become a proficient gift giver. In fact, it is one of the easiest love languages to learn.

IF YOU DISCOVER that your spouse's primary love language is receiving gifts, then perhaps you will understand that purchasing gifts for him or her is the best investment you can make. You are investing in your relationship and filling your love's emotional love tank, and with a full love tank, he or she will likely reciprocate emotional love to you in a language you will understand. When both persons' emotional needs are met, your marriage will take on a whole new dimension. Don't worry about your savings. You will always be a saver, but to invest in loving your spouse is to invest in blue chip stocks.

Physical presence in the
time of crisis is the most
powerful gift you can give
if your spouse's primary love
language is receiving gifts.

f the physical presence of your spouse is important to you, I urge you to verbalize that to your spouse. Don't expect him to read your mind. If, on the other hand, your spouse says to you, "I really want you to be there with me tonight, tomorrow, this afternoon," take his request seriously. From your perspective, it may not be important. But if you are not responsive to that request, you may be communicating a message you do not intend.

A husband once said, "When my mother died, my wife's supervisor said that she could be off two hours for the funeral but she needed to be back in the office for the afternoon. My wife told him that she felt her husband needed her support that day and she would have to be away the entire day. The supervisor replied, 'If you are gone all day, you may well lose your job.' My wife said, 'My husband is more important than my job.' She spent the day with me. Somehow that day, I felt more loved by her than ever before. I have never forgotten what she did."

Acts of service involve doing things you know your spouse would like you to do. You seek to please her by serving her, to express your love for her by doing things for her.

Such actions as cooking a meal, setting a table, washing dishes, vacuuming, cleaning a commode, getting hairs out of the sink, removing the white spots from the mirror, getting bugs off the windshield, taking out the garbage, changing the baby's diaper, painting a bedroom, dusting the bookcase, keeping the car in operating condition, washing or vacuuming the car, cleaning the garage, mowing the grass, trimming the shrubs, raking the leaves,

Service

dusting the blinds, walking the dog, changing the cat's litter box, and changing water in the goldfish bowl are all acts of service. They require thought, planning, time, effort, and energy. If done with a positive spirit, they are indeed expressions of love.

*L*ove is a choice and cannot be coerced. Criticism and demands tend to drive wedges. With enough criticism, you may get acquiescence from your spouse. He may do what you want, but probably it will not be an expression of love. You can give guidance to love by making requests: "I wish you would wash the car, change the baby's diaper, mow the grass," but you cannot create the will to love. Each of us must decide daily to love or not to love our spouses. If we choose to love, then expressing it in the way in which our spouse requests will make our love most effective emotionally.

Requests give direction to

Your Gift of Love

love, but demands stop
the flow of love.

MY SPOUSE'S CRITICISMS about my
behavior provide me with the clearest clue
to her primary love language. People tend
to criticize their spouse most loudly in the
area where they themselves have the
deepest emotional need. Their criticism
is an ineffective way of pleading for love.
If we understand that, it may help us
process their criticism in a more
productive manner. A wife may say to
her husband after he gives her a criticism,
"It sounds like that is extremely important
to you. Could you explain why it is so
crucial?" Criticism often needs clarifi-
cation. Initiating such a conversation
may eventually turn the criticism into a
request rather than a demand.

BEFORE THE DAYS of television, a person's idea of what a husband or wife should do and how they should relate was influenced primarily by one's own parents. With the pervasiveness of television and the proliferation of single-parent families, however, role models are often influenced by forces outside the home. Whatever your perceptions, chances are your spouse perceives marital roles somewhat differently than you do. A willingness to examine and change stereotypes is necessary in order to express love more effectively. Remember, there are no rewards for maintaining stereotypes. But there are tremendous benefits to meeting the emotional needs of your spouse.

7 Physical Touch

We have long known that physical touch is a way of communicating emotional love. Numerous research projects in the area of child development have made that conclusion: babies who are held, hugged, and kissed develop a healthier emotional life than those who are left for long periods of time without physical contact.

Physical touch is also a powerful vehicle for communicating marital love. Holding hands, kissing, embracing, and sexual intercourse are all ways of communicating emotional love to one's spouse. For some individuals, physical touch is their primary love language. Without it, they feel unloved. With it, their emotional tank is filled, and they feel secure in the love of their spouse.

To the person whose primary love language is physical touch, the message will be far louder than the words "I hate you" or "I love you." In marriage, the touch of love may take many forms. Since touch receptors are located throughout the body, lovingly touching your spouse almost anywhere can be an expression of love. That does not mean that all touches are created equal. Some will bring more pleasure to your spouse than others. Your best instructor is your spouse, of course.

Love touches may be implicit and require only a moment, such as putting your hand on his shoulder as you pour a cup of coffee. Explicit love touches obviously take more time, not only in actual touching but in developing your understanding of how to communicate love to your spouse this way. If a back massage communicates love loudly to your spouse, then the time, money, and energy you spend in learning to be a good masseur or masseuse will be well invested. Implicit love touches require little time but much thought, especially if physical touch is not your primary love language and if you did not grow up in a "touching family." Sitting close to each other on the couch as you watch your favorite television program requires no additional time but may communicate your love loudly. Touching your spouse as you walk through the room where he is sitting takes only a moment, but will speak volumes to your spouse.

Physical touch can make or break a relationship. It can communicate hate or love.

ONCE YOU DISCOVER that physical touch is the primary love language of your spouse, you are limited only by your imagination on ways to express love. Coming up with new ways and places to touch can be an exciting challenge. If you have not been an "under-the-table-toucher," you might find that it will add a spark to your dining out. If you are not accustomed to holding hands in public, you may find that you can fill your spouse's emotional love tank as you stroll through the parking lot.

If you don't normally kiss as soon as you get into the car together, you may find that it will greatly enhance your travels. Hugging your spouse before she goes shopping may not only express love, it may bring her home sooner. Try new touches in new places and let your spouse give you feedback on whether he finds it pleasurable or not. Remember, he or she has the final word. You are learning to speak his or her language.

ALMOST INSTINCTIVELY in a time of crisis, we hug one another. Why? Because physical touch is a powerful communicator of love. In a time of crisis, more than anything, we need to feel loved. We cannot always change events, but we can survive if we feel loved.

All marriages will experience crises. The death of parents is inevitable. Automobile accidents cripple and kill thousands each year. Disease is no respecter of persons. Disappointments are a part of life. The most important thing you can do for your mate in a time of crisis is to love him or her. If your spouse's primary love language is physical touch, nothing is more important than holding her as she cries. Your words may mean little, but your physical touch will communicate that you care. Crises provide a unique opportunity for expressing love. Your tender touches will be remembered long after the crisis has passed.

What is your primary love language? What makes you feel most loved by your spouse? What do you desire above all else? If the answer to those questions does not leap to your mind immediately, perhaps it will help to look at the negative use of love languages. What does your spouse do or say or fail to do or say that hurts you deeply? If, for example, your deepest pain is the critical, judgmental words of your spouse, then perhaps your love language is "Words of Affirmation." If your primary love language is used negatively by your spouse—that is, he does the opposite—it will hurt you more deeply than it would hurt someone else because

Love Language?

not only is he neglecting to speak your primary love language, he is actually using that language as a knife to your heart.

*A*nother way to discover your primary love language is to examine what you do or say to express love to your spouse. Chances are what you are doing for her is what you wish she would do for you. If you are constantly doing "Acts of Service" for your spouse, perhaps (although not always) that is your love language. If "Words of Affirmation" speak love to you, chances are you will use them in speaking love to your spouse. Thus,

You may discover your own

"How do I consciously

Your Gift of Love

you may discover your own language by asking, "How do I consciously express my love to my spouse?" But remember, that approach is only a possible clue to your love language; it is not an absolute indicator. For example, the husband who learned from his father to express love to his wife by giving her nice gifts expresses his love to his wife by doing what his father did, yet "Receiving Gifts" is not his primary love language. He is simply doing what he was trained to do by his father.

language by asking,

express my love to my spouse?"

TWO KINDS OF PEOPLE may have difficulty discovering their primary love language. The first is the individual whose emotional love tank has been full for a long time. Her spouse has expressed love in many ways, and she is not certain which of those ways makes her feel most loved. She simply knows that she is loved. The second is the individual whose love tank has been empty for so long that he doesn't remember what makes him feel loved. In either case, if you can go back to the experience of falling in love and ask yourself, "What did I like about my spouse in those days? What did he do or say that made me desire to be with him?" If you can conjure up those memories, it will give you some idea of your primary love language. Another approach would be to ask yourself, "What would be an ideal spouse to me? If I could have the perfect mate, what would she be like?" Your picture of a perfect mate should give you some idea of your primary love language.

PLAY THE FOLLOWING GAME three times a

week for three weeks. The game is called "Tank Check,"

and it is played like this. When you come home, one of

you says to the other, "On a scale of zero to ten, how is

your love tank tonight?" Zero means empty, and 10

means "I am full of love and can't handle any more." You

give a reading on your emotional love tank—10, 9, 8, 7,

6, 5, 4, 3, 2, 1, or 0, indicating how full it is. Your spouse

says, "What could I do to help fill it?" Then you make a

suggestion—something you would like your spouse to do

or say that evening. To the best of his ability, he will

respond to your request. Then you repeat the process in

the reverse order so that both of you have the

opportunity to do a reading on your love tank and to

make a suggestion toward filling it. If you play the

game for three weeks, you will be hooked on it, and it

can be a playful way of stimulating love expressions in

your marriage.

9 Choose to Love

How can we speak each other's love language when we are full of hurt, anger, and resentment over past failures? The answer to that question lies in the essential nature of our humanity. We are creatures of choice. That means that we have the capacity to make poor choices, which all of us have done. We have spoken critical words, and we have done hurtful things. We are not proud of those choices, although they may have seemed justified at the moment. Poor choices in the past don't mean that we must make them in the future. Instead we can say, "I'm sorry. I know I have hurt you, but I would like to make the future different. I would like to love you in your language. I would like to meet your needs." I have seen marriages rescued from the brink of divorce when couples make the choice to love.

Meeting my spouse's need for love is a choice I make each day. If I know her primary love language and choose to speak it, her deepest emotional need will be met and she will feel secure in my love.

If I learn the emotional love language of my spouse and speak it frequently, she will continue to feel loved. When she comes down from the obsession of the "in love experience," she will hardly even miss it because her emotional love tank will continue to be filled. However, if I have not learned her primary love language or have chosen not to speak it, when she descends from the emotional high, she will have the natural yearnings of unmet emotional need.

Meeting my wife's need for love is a choice I make each day. If I know her primary love language and choose to speak it, her deepest emotional need will be met and she will feel secure in my love. If she does the same for me, my emotional needs are met and both of us live with a full tank. In a state of emotional contentment, both of us will give our creative energies to many wholesome projects outside the marriage while we continue to keep our marriage exciting and growing.

*W*HEN AN ACTION DOESN'T COME NATURALLY TO YOU, IT IS A GREATER EXPRESSION OF LOVE.

"WHAT IF THE LOVE LANGUAGE of your

spouse is something that doesn't come naturally for

you?" When an action doesn't come naturally to you, it

is a greater expression of love. My wife knows that when

I vacuum the house, it's nothing but 100 percent pure,

unadulterated love. Someone says, "But, that's different. I

know that my spouse's love language is physical touch,

and I am not a toucher. I never saw my mother and

father hug each other. They never hugged me; I am just

not a toucher."

Love is something you do for someone else, not

something you do for yourself. Most of us do many

things each day that do not come "naturally" for us. The same is true with love. We discover the primary love language of our spouse, and we choose to speak it whether or not it is natural for us. We are not claiming to have warm, excited feelings. We are simply choosing to do it for his or her benefit. We want to meet our spouse's emotional need, and we reach out to speak his love language. In so doing, his emotional love tank is filled and chances are he will reciprocate and speak our language. When he does our emotions return, and our love tank begins to fill. Love is a choice. And either partner can start the process today.

10 The Rewards

My sense of self-worth is fed by the fact that my spouse loves me. After all, if he/she loves me, I must be worth loving. My parents may have given me negative or mixed messages about my worth, but my spouse knows me as an adult and loves me. Her love builds my self-esteem. The need for significance is the emotional force behind much of our behavior. Life is driven by the desire for success. We want our lives to count for something. We have our own idea of what it means to be significant, and we work hard to reach our goals. Feeling loved by a spouse enhances our sense of significance. We reason, *If someone loves me, I must have significance.*

# of Love

The need
for love is
our deepest
emotional
need, and when that need is
being met, we tend to respond
positively to the person who is
meeting it.

When my spouse lovingly invests time, energy, and effort in me, I believe that I am significant. Without love, I may spend a lifetime in search of significance, self-worth, and security. When I experience love, it impacts all of those needs positively. I am now freed to develop my potential. I am more secure in my self-worth and can now turn my efforts outward instead of being obsessed with my own needs. True love always liberates.

Love is not the answer to everything, but it creates a climate of security in which we can seek answers to those things that bother us. In the security of love, a couple can discuss differences without condemnation. Conflicts can be resolved. Two people who are different can learn to live together in harmony. We discover how to bring out the best in each other. Those are the rewards of love. The decision to love your spouse

holds tremendous potential.
Learning his/her primary love
language makes that potential
a reality. Love really does
"make the world go round."

11 Love in Action

For most wives, the desire to be sexually intimate with their husbands grows out of a sense of being loved by their husbands. If they feel loved, then they desire sexual intimacy. If they do not feel loved, they likely feel used in the sexual context. That is why loving someone who is not loving you is extremely difficult. It goes against our natural tendencies. You will probably have to rely heavily upon your faith in God in order to do this. Perhaps it will help if you read Jesus' sermon on loving your enemies, loving those who hate you, loving those who use you. And then ask God to help you practice the teachings of Jesus.

Perhaps it would be helpful for us to distinguish between love as a feeling and love as an action. If you claim to have feelings that you do not have, that is hypo-critical and such false communication is not the way to build intimate relationships. But if you express an act of love that is designed for the other person's benefit or pleasure, it is simply a choice.

IF YOU CLAIM TO HAVE FEELINGS THAT YOU DO NOT HAVE, THAT IS HYPOCRITICAL. BUT IF YOU EXPRESS AN ACT OF LOVE THAT IS DESIGNED FOR THE OTHER PERSON'S BENEFIT OR PLEASURE, IT IS SIMPLY A CHOICE.

erhaps you need a miracle in your marriage. Tell your spouse that you have been thinking about your marriage and have decided that you would like to do a better job of meeting his/her needs. Ask for suggestions on how you could improve. His suggestions will be a clue to his primary love language. If he makes no suggestions, guess his love language based on the things he has complained about over the years. Then, for six months, focus your attention on that love language. At the end of each month, ask your spouse for feedback on how you are doing and for further suggestions.

miracle worker!

Whenever your spouse indicates that he is seeing improvement, wait one week and then make a specific request. The request should be something you really want him to do for you. If he chooses to do it, you will know that he is responding to your needs. If he does not honor your request, continue to love him. Maybe next month he will respond positively. If your spouse starts speaking your love language by responding to your requests, your positive emotions toward him will return, and in time your marriage will be reborn.

12 A Personal

We each come to marriage with a different personality and history. We bring emotional baggage into our marriage relationship. We come with different expectations, different ways of approaching things, and different opinions about what matters in life. In a healthy marriage, we need not agree on everything, but we must find a way to handle our differences so that they do not become divisive. With empty love tanks, couples tend to argue and withdraw, and some may tend to be violent verbally or physically in their arguments. But when the love tank is full, we create a climate of friendliness, a climate that seeks to understand, that is willing to allow differences and to negotiate problems. I am convinced that no single area of marriage affects the rest of marriage as much as meeting the emotional need for love.

I dream of a day when the potential of the married couples in this country can be unleashed for the good of humankind, when husbands and wives can live life with full emotional love tanks and reach out to accomplish their potential as individuals and as couples. I dream of a day when children can grow up in homes filled with love and security, where children's developing energies can be channeled to learning and serving rather than seeking the love they did not receive at home. It is my desire that this brief volume will kindle the flame of love in your marriage and in the marriages of thousands of other couples like you.

13 Love Notes

* Recall a time when you attempted to communicate love, but your efforts were not received. Were your expressions rejected or simply not recognized? Why do you think your sincere expressions failed to communicate your heart?

* An empty love tank is like running your car engine without oil. What are some specific things that you can do to help keep the love tank full in your relationship with your spouse?

* Think of three shared experiences that brought you and your marriage partner closer. How did these experiences involve quality time in shared activities? Plan a new event that has great "memory" potential.

* Think of some of the gifts that you have given your spouse. Which gifts have been most appreciated? Plan to give some token (no matter how small) of your love each week for the next month.

* Physical touch, as a gesture of love, is a powerful form of communication, from the smallest touch to the most passionate kiss. Attempt to share openly with your spouse those touches that are most meaningful and pleasurable to you.

* Play the "Love Tank Check" game over the next month. Ask your spouse, "On the basis of zero to ten, where would you rate our relationship?" Ask your spouse for suggestions as to how you might raise that number and then get busy!

* List three things you have said or done toward your spouse within the past month that expressed your love while seeking the best for your spouse.

Your Gift of Love

*True love seeks to give more than it gets. Think of some of your recent expressions of love. What did you expect in return? This week, focus on what your spouse might expect in return for expressions of love given to you.

* Make a list of things you and your spouse appreciate about each other. This week, try to express at least two compliments to each other based on your lists.

* This month, choose three simple but humble chores that you don't especially enjoy, but that your spouse would be pleased to see completed. Surprise your spouse by doing them without being asked.

Your Gift of Love

"for more information

on building a strong

loving relationship..."

MARRIAGES MAY BE MADE IN HEAVEN, but they are nurtured here on earth. In the best-selling book, *The Five Love Languages*, author and marriage counselor Gary Chapman explains how people communicate love in different ways. If you express love in a way your spouse doesn't understand, he or she won't realize you've expressed your love at all. The problem is that you're speaking two different languages. *The Five Love Languages*, explores the all-important languages of love, in depth, helping each partner discover which actions are interpreted by the other as loving and affirming, and which as indifferent and demeaning.

For partners seeking harmony, how we express ourselves is as important as what we say. Read *The Five Love Languages* and discover how to express heartfelt commitment to your mate. Before you know it, you'll learn to speak and understand the unique languages of love and effectively express your love as well as feel truly loved in return!

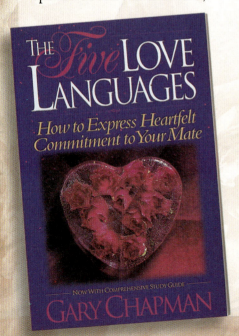